D0517599

TABLE OF CONTENTS

PUBLISHING THE NEWSPAPER

INTRODUCTION

Welcome to the world of newspaper writing! Use these activities in class and students will gain experience in newspaper production from start to finish. The easy-to-follow lessons venture through prewriting, writing, editing, proofreading, typesetting, layout, and end with actual newspaper production. Each activity can be done with paper and pencil or it can be quickly adapted to computer production. You may even choose to use a combination of paper-pencil and computer work. Use the reproducible page for first drafts and then have students keyboard and format their final drafts on the computer. Certainly, because of easy access to multiple fonts and page structures, the computer will enhance the actual publication of the newspaper. It is like magic to simply choose a two-column format and click to see it implemented! Use the resources that are appropriate and available to your students as they produce a class newspaper. Students will thrill to see their work in print, and parents and administrators will love to hear what's going on in the classroom.

This program provides three to four weeks of newspaper experiences for middle grades students at any skill level. As soon as students are able to put a few words to paper, this program becomes effective. With so many states requiring essay writing exams at various levels, teachers are anxious to find new ways to increase writing skills. This program is just the ticket to improved writing, thinking, and communicating skills necessary in our technological and information-driven age. It can be easily adapted for either small group or individual use, and each individual student or group can create a newspaper of their very own.

Every student should complete each activity in this workbook, although every completed activity will not be published. (When the editing process has been completed, everyone will have something in the newspaper. This decision-making process is discussed in the "Publishing" section.) Each day, encourage students to share what they have written.

What follows is your step-by-step guide for using this program. No time recommendations are given, since the length of the lessons depends upon the number and ability level of the students involved. Each lesson includes prewriting activities, as well as modifications for writing across the curriculum. You may adapt these lessons for a social studies, science, or math emphasis. The program can also be easily adapted for foreign language use and other courses of study. Also included are reproducible worksheets on which students can write notes, rough drafts, and final newspaper stories.

Please allow your students plenty of room for individuality during these lessons. Looking at situations from different points of view and explaining material in different ways enhances a journalistic experience. Let your students' creative juices run freely, and you will be surprised at their ability. Allow for humor as often as they will provide it! Use the lessons in isolation or as a total program. There are no rules—only the limits of your students' imaginations and their desire for new experiences.

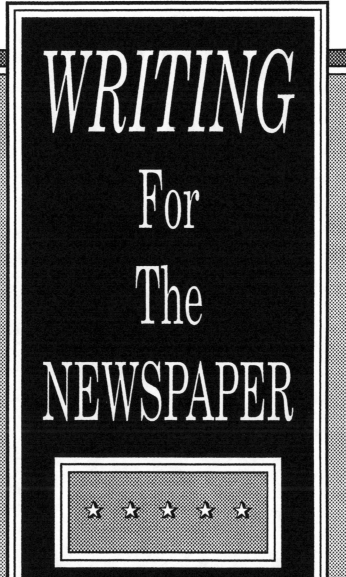

WRITING
For
The
NEWSPAPER

★ ★ ★ ★ ★

Globeman's News

NEWS FEATURES

OBJECTIVE:

Students will write news stories based on real or fictitious events. Students will gain experience in organizing their ideas, summarizing information, and synthesizing a wide range of facts into a cohesive whole.

PREWRITING:

Using the "Who, What, Where, When, and Why" method of reporting, students will complete the News Feature Notes worksheet on pages 11–12. Students can write about an actual event, an imaginary event, or an event from a work of literature you are currently reading. Each student will write the final draft of his or her news story on a copy of the worksheet on page 13.

INTEGRATING THE CURRICULUM

SOCIAL STUDIES:

Students can write their news features about a historical event.

SCIENCE:

Recent scientific discoveries or lab experiments your students have completed can be used as material for news features.

MATH:

Events from math class or articles on the economy make good math-based news stories.

NEWS FEATURE NOTES

Write the notes for your news feature on this sheet.

What happened? _____

_____

_____

_____

_____

_____

_____

_____

_____

Who was involved? _____

_____

_____

_____

_____

_____

_____

Where did it happen? _____

_____

_____

_____

_____

_____

_____

Name _____

When did the event begin and end? _____
_____
_____
_____

Why did this happen? _____
_____
_____
_____
_____
_____
_____

What were the results? _____
_____
_____
_____
_____
_____
_____
_____

What might happen next? _____
_____
_____
_____
_____
_____
_____

Name _____

NEWS FEATURE DRAFT

HEADLINE:

BY:

Write the draft of your news story on this sheet.

_____
_____
_____
_____
_____
_____
_____
_____
_____
_____
_____
_____
_____
_____
_____
_____
_____
_____
_____
_____
_____
_____
_____

Name _____

SPORTS FEATURES

OBJECTIVE:

Students will write a feature story covering a sporting event, either real or imagined. Students will gain experience in using colorful language, organizing their ideas, and summarizing information.

PREWRITING:

Read aloud to the class a sports story from your local newspaper, preferably covering an event from your school system. Then make a list on the board of the different sporting events which are covered by newspapers. Don't neglect less publicized sports, such as bowling, swimming, and archery. These ideas will help students decide which sporting events they wish to cover. Whether writing about a real or imaginary event, each student will follow the outline on page 15 to organize his or her story prior to writing a draft on a copy of the worksheet on page 16. Stress the use of exciting and colorful language when writing sports features.

INTEGRATING THE CURRICULUM

SOCIAL STUDIES:

Instruct students to write about sporting events applicable to certain periods of time or countries, such as jousting (Middle Ages) or cricket (England).

SCIENCE:

Play-by-plays of science experiments can be used in lieu of sports events.

MATH:

Sports stories usually stress statistics, times, and scores. Emphasize the importance of math when writing about and analyzing these figures.

SPORTS FEATURE NOTES

Use this worksheet to make notes about the sporting event which you are covering. Use extra paper if necessary.

Name of event: _____

Where did it take place? _____

_____

_____

When did it take place? _____

_____

_____

Who (teams or individuals) was involved? _____

_____

_____

_____

_____

_____

Scores or results of event: _____

_____

_____

_____

Highlights of event: _____

_____

_____

_____

_____

Upcoming event: _____

_____

_____

_____

Name _____

SPORTS FEATURE DRAFT

Write the draft of your sports story on this sheet.

_____
_____
_____
_____
_____
_____
_____
_____
_____
_____
_____
_____
_____
_____
_____
_____
_____
_____
_____
_____
_____
_____
_____
_____
_____
_____
_____

Name _____

INTERVIEWS

OBJECTIVE:

Students will interview another person and write a profile about that person.

PREWRITING:

Students interview either a person outside of the class or a classmate. Once the subject has been identified, students use the interview questions on pages 18–19 to spur conversation with the subject. More questions can, of course, be added. Students will then use their notes to write a personality profile draft on a copy of the worksheet on page 20.

INTEGRATING THE CURRICULUM

SOCIAL STUDIES:

Students can pretend to be historical figures and answer the questions asked of them from that figure's point of view.

SCIENCE:

Students can pretend to be animals, plants, or famous scientists, and then answer the questions asked of them from that individual's point of view.

MATH:

Students can interview math teachers, bankers, accountants, or other people working in math-related careers.

INTERVIEW FOR PERSONALITY PROFILE

Everyone is interesting!

Ask your interview subject the following questions. Feel free to add questions of your own, but avoid questions that prompt only a "yes" or "no" response.

What is your background? _____

_____

_____

_____

_____

_____

Tell me about your family. _____

_____

_____

_____

_____

_____

_____

Describe the activities in which you are currently involved. _____

_____

_____

_____

_____

_____

Tell me about something unusual that has happened to you. _____

_____

_____

_____

_____

_____

Name _____

Name one thing about which you feel strongly. _____

_____

_____

_____

Why do you feel strongly about that? _____

_____

_____

_____

_____

_____

_____

_____

_____

_____

_____

_____

_____

_____

If you could say one thing about yourself, what would it be? _____

_____

_____

_____

_____

_____

_____

_____

_____

_____

_____

Name _____

PERSONALITY PROFILE DRAFT

HEADLINE:

BY:

Write the draft of your personality profile on this sheet.

_____
_____
_____
_____
_____
_____
_____
_____
_____
_____
_____
_____
_____
_____
_____
_____
_____
_____
_____
_____
_____
_____
_____
_____

Name _____

EDITORIALS

OBJECTIVE:

Students will write persuasive opinion essays. Students will gain experience in expressing their opinions in a formal setting.

PREWRITING:

Distribute copies of the prewriting planner on pages 22 and 23. Allow students several minutes to write their first thoughts about each starter statement. After a few minutes, ask some students to share their ideas. Then each student should pick one of the prompts and write a complete editorial draft on a copy of the worksheet on page 24.

INTEGRATING THE CURRICULUM

SOCIAL STUDIES:

Instead of using the prewriting worksheet on pages 22 and 23, write several starter statements on the board using social studies concepts, such as "If I were President . . ." " . . . is the greatest country in the world, because . . ." and "War is . . ."

SCIENCE:

Instead of using the prewriting worksheet on pages 22 and 23, write several science-based starter statements on the board. Sample statements include, "If I lived on Mars . . ." and "Earth will soon . . ."

MATH:

Instead of using the prewriting worksheet on pages 22 and 23, write several math-based starter statements on the board. Sample statements include "Is math really necessary?" and "Calculators should be . . ."

EDITORIAL WRITING NOTES

Complete the following starter statements with your own ideas. Choose one of these to complete as your editorial essay.

What this school needs is _____

_____

_____

_____

_____

_____

_____

War is _____

_____

_____

_____

_____

_____

_____

_____

Our earth is about to _____

_____

_____

_____

_____

_____

_____

_____

Name _____

I think _____

should be abolished because _____

_____

_____

_____

_____

_____

_____

_____

If I were President, I would _____

_____

_____

_____

_____

_____

_____

_____

_____

I believe in _____

_____

_____

_____

_____

_____

_____

_____

_____

Name _____

EDITORIAL DRAFT

HEADLINE:

BY:

Write the draft of your editorial on this sheet.

Name _____

MOVIE REVIEWS

OBJECTIVE:

Students will write a subjective critique of a movie they have seen recently. Students will gain experience in making an analysis and expressing their opinions in a formal setting.

PREWRITING:

List several popular movie titles on the board. Student volunteers can orally give their opinions of the movies. After a class discussion of movies, each student will critique a movie seen recently for which he or she has a strong like or dislike. Each student should first complete the notes worksheet on a copy of page 26. The movie review draft should be written on a copy of page 27.

INTEGRATING THE CURRICULUM

SOCIAL STUDIES:

Students can critique an educational film they have seen in class or a commercial film that takes place in another country or historical time setting.

SCIENCE:

Students can critique an educational film based on scientific concepts.

MATH:

Students can critique an educational film based on mathematical concepts.

MOVIE REVIEW NOTES

Answer these questions about a movie you have recently seen that you really liked or disliked. Use this worksheet to write the notes for your movie review.

Movie title: _____

Actors and actresses: _____
_____
_____

Your opinion of the performance of the actors and actresses: _____
_____
_____
_____
_____

Summary of the story: _____
_____
_____
_____
_____
_____
_____

When and where the movie takes place: _____
_____
_____

Theme or moral of the movie: _____
_____
_____

Intended audience (Circle One):   G   PG   PG-13   R

Your opinion (Does the film achieve its intended goals?): _____
_____
_____

I give this move a rating of   *   **   ***   **** *(one star=terrible, four stars=great)*

Name _____

MOVIE REVIEW DRAFT

HEADLINE:

BY:

Write the draft of your movie review on this sheet.

_____
_____
_____
_____
_____
_____
_____
_____
_____
_____
_____
_____
_____
_____
_____
_____
_____
_____
_____
_____
_____
_____

Name _____

OBJECTIVE:

Students will create original picture poems and haiku.

PREWRITING:

Create your own picture poem and haiku and write them on the board (samples are shown on pages 29 and 30). Explain that picture poems are created by designing the words of the poem into a simple picture that illustrates the poem's theme. Often the picture adds an extra "punch" to the words, as in a picture poem about the dangers of drugs being drawn in the shape of a skull and crossbones. Haiku is a form of Japanese poetry, and its subject is usually nature. A haiku has a one-word title followed by three lines (seven syllables in the first and third lines and five syllables in the second line). After introducing these two forms of poetry, students can then use copies of the worksheets on pages 29 and 30 to create their own picture poems and haiku. These poems can be clipped and placed directly onto a layout sheet. Advanced students can use these short poems as a springboard to write more lengthy works of poetry, if desired.

INTEGRATING THE CURRICULUM

SOCIAL STUDIES:

Picture poems can be written in the shapes of states, countries, or social symbols. Haiku may be modified to cover social studies chapter themes or written from the point of view of a person in a particular historical time period.

SCIENCE:

Picture poems can illustrate any scientific concept being studied. Modify definition of haiku to extend to any science concept currently being studied.

MATH:

Picture poems can take the shape of geometric figures, numbers, or designs. Haiku can be modified by using a math theme.

POETRY DRAFT (PICTURE POEM)

A picture poem is a poem which uses a few simple words that are written in the shape of an object which illustrates the meaning of the poem. Look at the sample, then try a couple of your own.

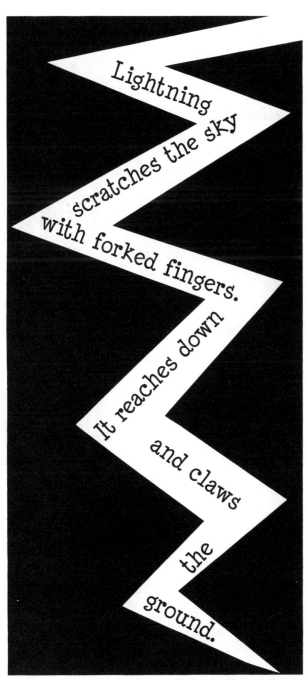

Lightning
scratches the sky
with forked fingers.
It reaches down
and claws
the
ground.

©1997 by Marjorie Frank.

POETRY DRAFT (HAIKU)

Haiku is a simple, but elegant, form of Japanese poetry. A haiku begins with a one-word title, usually concerning nature. The poem consists of only three lines. The first has seven syllables; the second line has five syllables; and the third line again has seven syllables. Study the sample below, then try a couple of your own.

* * * Snow * * *

Gently tumbling flakes of white

Drifting crystals fall

Winter's blanket coats the ground

One word title _____

Seven syllables_____

Five syllables _____

Seven syllables _____

* * * * *

Now write another here:

Name _____

ADVICE COLUMN

OBJECTIVE:

Students will write letters to the advice columnist and answer the letters of other students.

PREWRITING:

Read aloud several actual advice column letters. In addition to newspaper columns, you may want to read some advice columns from teen magazines. Using copies of the worksheet on page 32, students write letters to "Gabby." Signatures on letters should reflect the problem, not the writer's name. When letters are completed, papers are collected and randomly distributed for answers to be written on copies of the worksheet on page 33.

INTEGRATING THE CURRICULUM:

SOCIAL STUDIES:

The writer can imagine him- or herself as a teenager in another place or time, think of the problems that person might face, and write about those problems. For example, how might an early American colonist have felt, or how might a teenager feel today in a war-torn country?

SCIENCE:

Letters can be written from the science student to "Mr. Science." Students can ask about concepts they don't understand. Answers can be funny or enlightening (teacher may have to help).

MATH:

Letters can concern math concepts, such as spending, loans, budgeting, or time.

ADVICE COLUMN LETTER

Dear Gabby,

_____
_____
_____
_____
_____
_____
_____
_____
_____
_____
_____
_____
_____
_____
_____
_____
_____
_____
_____
_____
_____
_____
_____

Signed,

_____

Name _____

ADVICE COLUMN RESPONSE

Now exchange papers with another student or turn in your paper to your teacher, who will distribute them. Now you are "Gabby," and you must write an answer to someone else's problem.

Dear _____ ,

(Use name from the signature of the letter to which you are responding.)

_____

_____

_____

_____

_____

_____

_____

_____

_____

_____

_____

_____

_____

_____

_____

_____

_____

_____

Signed,

Gabby

Name _____

 # COMIC STRIP

OBJECTIVE:

Students will create original comic strips.

PREWRITING:

PART ONE: This activity will familiarize students with the idea of creating a storyboard for drawing a comic strip. Bring several section of Sunday comics or daily comic strips pages to class. Each student will choose one comic strip panel. Have them notice how the pictures tell a story with just a few words. The pictures also give the reader clues about characterization and setting. Reproduce the grid on page 35 for students. Have students note the information the cartoonist included in each frame. They should focus not only on the storyline, but also on setting and characterization.

PART TWO: Using a copy of the worksheet on page 36, each student will create a character about whom they would like to draw a four-panel cartoon. Students can create animals, super-hero characters, or any other original character. Students should complete the prewriting questions found on the top of page 36, and then draw their comic strips in the panels on the bottom of the page. The panels on the bottom of page 36 may be clipped or scanned to use in the final copy of the newspaper.

INTEGRATING THE CURRICULUM

SOCIAL STUDIES:

Set panels in a foreign country or use historical figures and events. You may also decide to bring to class examples of political cartoons and instruct students to depict current political events in a similar style.

SCIENCE:

Characters can be microscopic organisms, parts of plants, or famous scientists making discoveries.

MATH:

Characters can be geometric figures, numbers, or students in a math class.

Choose the first four frames of a comic strip. Look at each frame. Record the information that the cartoonist gives the reader in each frame. Include information about the storyline, characterization, and setting.

COMIC STRIP DRAFT

Invent an original comic strip character. Your character can be an ordinary person, super-hero, or anyone else! Complete the information below, then create an episode.

Character name: _____

His or her occupation: _____

Special skills or powers: _____

_____

_____

Enemies, if any: _____

_____

_____

Friends and family: _____

_____

_____

Setting of comic strip: _____

_____

_____

Draw the expressions of your character in the panels below:

Happy Face	Sad Face	Angry Face

Draw an episode of your comic strip in the panels below:

Name _____

BIRTH ANNOUNCEMENTS AND OBITUARIES

OBJECTIVE ONE:

Students will learn how to write birth announcements. This activity will sharpen students' summarization and research skills.

PREWRITING:

Display birth announcements from a local newspaper. Students will create imaginary birth announcements after completing the starter statements at the top of page 38. (ALTERNATE ACTIVITY: Research the births of famous people and write their birth announcements.) After completing notes (or research), each student writes the draft of his or her announcement on the bottom of the worksheet (page 38). Each student then writes his or her own birth announcement on a copy of the worksheet on page 39.

INTEGRATING THE CURRICULUM

SOCIAL STUDIES: Use famous historical figures as birth announcement subjects.

SCIENCE: Write announcements for famous scientists or animals (dinosaurs or vanishing species).

MATH: To place emphasis on math, stress birth weights and times of birth.

OBJECTIVE TWO:

Students will write obituaries for people from the past, real or imaginary, historical or fictional. This activity will sharpen students' summarization and research skills.

PREWRITING:

List on the board names of literary characters, authors (deceased), or other notables from the past. Each student will research a person's life and death using encyclopedias or other reference materials. Information on fictional characters can be reviewed by reading the story of which they are a part. (Information can also be purely imaginary.) Each student will then use a copy of the worksheet on page 40 on which to write the obituary. After completing this activity, have each student make up his or her own obituary on a copy of the worksheet on page 41.

INTEGRATING THE CURRICULUM

SOCIAL STUDIES: Use historical figures from certain periods of history or particular countries. Local personalities can also be used.

SCIENCE: Use famous scientists as obituary subjects.

MATH: Students can write obituaries for the ancient philosophers and fathers of mathematical theories.

BIRTH ANNOUNCEMENT DRAFT

Choose a famous person, character from literature, or create someone from your imagination, and write a birth announcement. If the person is real, do enough research to find out the following information. If imaginary, just make it up! Write the draft of your announcement in the box below.

Name of baby: _____

Mother's name: _____

Father's name: _____

Place of birth: _____

Date of birth: _____   Time of birth: _____

Weight and length of baby (if available): _____

Brothers and sisters: _____

_____

_____

Name _____

BIRTH ANNOUNCEMENT DRAFT (YOUR OWN)

Do some research to find out the following information about yourself. Then write the draft of your birth announcement on the bottom of the worksheet.

Name of baby: _____

Mother's name: _____

Father's name: _____

Place of birth: _____

Date of birth: _____ Time of birth: _____

Weight and length of baby (if available): _____

Brothers and sisters: _____

_____

_____

Name _____

OBITUARY DRAFT
(FAMOUS PERSON)

Choose a famous character, real or imaginary. After researching (or inventing information), write your obituary notes on this worksheet. Also fill in the information on the tombstone.

HERE LIES

_____

Born _____

Died _____

Services were held for _____,

who died on _____ at the age of _____.

The deceased was born on _____ in the town of _____,

the (son, daughter) of _____.

The deceased was known for _____

_____

_____.

(He or she) is survived by the following relatives: _____

_____

_____

_____

Name _____

OBITUARY DRAFT
(YOUR OWN)

Write your own obituary in the space provided below.

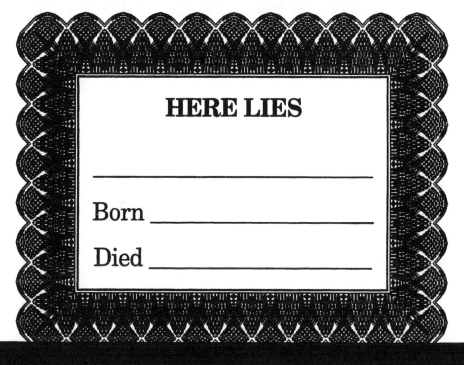

HERE LIES

_____

Born _____

Died _____

Services were held for _____,

who died on _____ at the age of _____.

The deceased was born on _____ in the town of _____,

the (son, daughter) of _____.

The deceased was known for _____

_____

_____.

(He or she) is survived by the following relatives: _____

_____

_____

_____

_____

_____

Name _____

WEDDING ANNOUNCEMENTS

OBJECTIVE:

Students will learn how to write wedding announcements.

PREWRITING:

Display wedding stories from a local newspaper. After noting their style and format, students will create imaginary wedding stories using the starter statements on page 43.

(ALTERNATE ACTIVITY: Students write about the weddings of famous people.)

The draft of the wedding announcement will be written on a copy of page 44.

INTEGRATING THE CURRICULUM

SOCIAL STUDIES:

Use famous historical figures as subjects of the wedding announcements.

SCIENCE:

Wedding announcements can be written for famous scientists (such as the Curies) or zoo animal pairs.

MATH:

Include at least ten numbers in the wedding announcement (example: three-tiered cake, fifteen-foot train).

WEDDING ANNOUNCEMENT NOTES

Choose a famous person, characters from literature, or create a couple from your imagination. Whether real or imaginary, have fun with this activity by creating the story as you wish.

Name of couple: _____

_____

Parents of the bride: _____

_____

Parents of the groom: _____

_____

Place and date of wedding: _____

_____

Pastor and wedding party: _____

_____

_____

Description of gowns and tuxedos (or suits): _____

_____

_____

_____

Decorations: _____

_____

_____

Reception: _____

_____

_____

Honeymoon destination: _____

Name _____

WEDDING ANNOUNCEMENT DRAFT

Write the draft of your wedding announcement on this sheet.

_____

_____

_____

_____

_____

_____

_____

_____

_____

_____

_____

_____

_____

_____

_____

_____

_____

_____

_____

_____

_____

_____

_____

_____

_____

_____

_____

_____

Name _____

OBJECTIVE:

Students will create, administer, interpret, and report results from a survey.

PREWRITING:

Each student will choose one question to ask to students, friends, or community members. The question, such as, "What is your favorite type of fast food?" should allow for several possible answers. Each student should collect answers from twenty-five people. When all of the answers are collected, each student will compile a list of answers, placing tally marks beside each response. The chart on the left-hand side of page 46 should be used to record answers and tallies. The totals for each answer can be used to compute percentages. (With twenty-five people surveyed, multiply each answer by four.) Report findings on the chart on the right-hand side of page 46. This chart (along with the survey question above it) can be cut and inserted directly onto the layout sheet for publication.

INTEGRATING THE CURRICULUM

SOCIAL STUDIES, SCIENCE AND MATH:

This activity already incorporates all of these subjects and can be used without modification, if desired.

SURVEY

Step One: Write a question that can have many possible answers, such as, "What is your favorite dessert?"

Step Two: Ask your question to twenty-five people. Write their answers in the first column on the left-hand side of the page. Place a tally mark in the second column each time the same answer is given. (When finished, you should have twenty-five marks.) Write totals in the third column.

Step Three: Multiply the totals by four. This gives you the percent of each answer. Write the answers and percentages in order from greatest to least on the chart on the right-hand side of the page. This is your chart to publish.

Your Survey Question: _____

_____

Answers Given	Tally Marks	Total
	Total	25

Survey Question: _____

_____

_____

Answers:	%
Total	100%

Name _____

PUZZLES AND GAMES

OBJECTIVE:

Students will create original word search or crossword puzzles.

PREWRITING:

On a scratch sheet of paper, each student should write a list of words (number of words at your discretion). Words may be based on a piece of literature read recently, any other theme, or no theme at all. Check for spelling accuracy. Reproduce a copy of page 48 for each student. Students will use this worksheet to write original word search or crossword puzzles. Students may write their words in the blocks vertically, horizontally, diagonally, and backwards. Once the words are plugged in, extra letters must be added. Used words must also be listed on the bottom of the page. Advanced students may decide to attempt crossword puzzles with "Across" and "Down" clues written on the bottom of the page. Keep several extra copies of the worksheet on hand as students may need to start over. (The larger grid on page 49 is for use with younger children. Depending on the number of pages in your newspaper, you can use this puzzle as is or reduce it on your school's copying machine.)

INTEGRATING THE CURRICULUM

SOCIAL STUDIES:

Students should use words from chapters in your social studies text. States and their capitals can also be used. Rather than words, significant dates can be hidden in a number search.

SCIENCE:

In addition to using words from science text chapters, students can use lists of words representing such topics as "elements" or "parts of the digestive system."

MATH:

Instead of letters, use numbers. Be sure that the student lists the correct numbers at the bottom of the page. Math problems can be listed on the bottom of the page with the answers hidden in the word search.

PUZZLE WORKSHEET I

Use one or both of these grids to create a word search or crossword puzzle. Write clues beneath the grids, and give each puzzle a title.

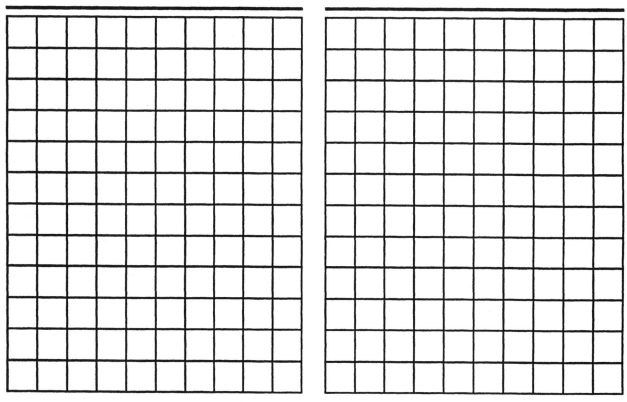

Clues:

Clues:

Name _____

 # PUZZLE WORKSHEET II

Create a word search or crossword puzzle in this grid. Remember to give your puzzle a title and write clues at the bottom of the page.

Clues:

Name _____

RECIPES

OBJECTIVE:

Students will write the preparation and cooking instructions for a favorite recipe.

PREWRITING:

Bring cookbooks and cooking magazines to class. Allow students to search through the books for recipes they like. Write out a typical recipe format on the board and discuss its layout with your class. (ALTERNATE ACTIVITY: Demonstrate a "no cook" recipe for the class with tasting privileges! Or ask students to bring in a favorite recipe from home, and share dishes with the class.) Reproduce copies of page 51 on which each student will write his or her favorite recipe.

INTEGRATING THE CURRICULUM

SOCIAL STUDIES:

Recipes can reflect the traditional cuisine of a country being studied or a particular period of history.

SCIENCE:

"Recipes" can be made for compounds or mixtures, rather than foods.

MATH:

Stress measurement and baking time. Have students double and half recipes before publishing them.

 ## RECIPE WORKSHEET

Write your favorite recipe here or create a wild and crazy one of your own!

Tell something interesting about this food: _____

_____

_____

_____

Title: _____

Amounts: Ingredients:

Oven temperature: _____

Steps of preparation: _____

_____

_____

_____

_____

_____

Cooking time: _____

How to serve: _____

_____

_____

Who taught you how to make this dish? _____

Name _____

ADVERTISEMENTS

OBJECTIVE:

Students will create their own newspaper ads.

PREWRITING:

Students should look through magazines and newspapers to find ads they find intriguing. Ask them, "What sorts of ads appeal to you the most?" While they are researching the ads, write a list of persuasive marketing words on the board (discount, new, improved, more, light, environmentally safe, great buy, cholesterol-free, fat-free, etc.). Explain how advertisers use propaganda techniques to sell products. Some of these include the use of analogy, the bandwagon approach, emotional appeal, exaggeration, generalizations, name dropping, and testimonials. Allow them to brainstorm to come up with examples of these and other sales techniques. Reproduce the list of fictitious product names on page 53 or make a transparency. Each student should choose or create five products for which they will write advertisements. Allow time for the ad design and have students submit their final designs on a copy of the worksheet on page 54.

INTEGRATING THE CURRICULUM

SOCIAL STUDIES:

Students can think of original products for a certain period of history or from a particular country. Then they can write the advertisement for the products.

SCIENCE:

Make a list of science-related equipment for students to advertise. For fun, let students advertise science text chapter concepts ("Spleens 'r' Us," "Bill's New and Used Batteries") or products from other planets.

MATH:

Use the fictitious products list on page 53, but have students stress price, discount, coupon values, and other consumer math concepts in their ads.

Mexicali Chili

Clean Sweep Window Cleaner

Rose Petal Shampoo

Sunny Morning Orange Juice

Bill's New and Used Dentures

True Blue Blueberry Jelly

Sure Strike Fish Lures

Jiggle Gelatin

Sweet Thing Snack Cakes

Peppy Popcorn

Neptune I (sports car)

Bright Toothpaste

Yum-Ice Frozen Treats

Mom's Cleaning Service

Sure Catch Rods and Reels

Snuggle-up Sleeping Bags

Great Timing Watches

Pep-up Vitamins

Blue Blazes BBQ Sauce

Chu's Oriental Rice Mix

Butter Melt Crackers

Rainbow Crayons

Puffy Marshmallows

Speed Demon Bikes

Good 'n' Creamy Peanut Butter

Scrubby Cleaner

Marshmallow Puffs Cereal

Easy-Cut Lawnmowers

Sweet Treat Raisins

Choco-Delight Cookies

Healthy Pet Dog Food

Fresh-Self Deodorant

Fizzle Cola

Zoom Skateboards

Cozy Feet Slippers

Pet Pest Flea Spray

Thunder Speakers

Fluff Shaving Cream

Sunshine Margarine

Superwrite Pencils

Sticky-Stuff Glue

Friendly Fred's Florist

Soak It Paper Towels

Race Track Shoes

Hunk o' Nuts Bar

Go-Juice Gasoline

Angel White Tissues

Donna's Studio of Dance

High-Tech Computers

Bright Glow Light Bulbs

Slim-You Cottage Cheese

Dates 'n' Stuff Fiber Cereal

Straight-A Notebook Paper

Granny's Oven Bread

Fudgy Wudgy Brownie Mix

Baby Face Make-Up

Sweet Tooth Artificial Sweetener

Deep Sea Tuna

Burger-Dog Fast Food

Grime-Away Detergent

AD LAYOUT

Create your advertisements in the boxes below. The top four boxes will make one-column ads. The large box at the bottom uses two columns.

Name _____

CLASSIFIED ADS AND FILLERS

CLASSIFIED ADS

OBJECTIVE ONE:

Each student will write several classified advertisements.

PREWRITING:

Have available the classified section of a large city's newspaper. Students should locate ads from three categories: for sale, wanted, and one other. Ask students to read the ads aloud. Point out the various abbreviations used in these ads. Students will then write their ads on the top portion of copies of the worksheet on page 56. One sample is given.

INTEGRATING THE CURRICULUM

SOCIAL STUDIES:

Classified ads can be written from a historical perspective or as if in another country's newspaper.

SCIENCE:

Classified ads can relate to chapter concepts ("Wanted: Two parts hydrogen seeks one part oxygen. Contact: Distilled Waters, Inc.").

MATH:

Classified ads can illustrate "missing parts" math problems. ("Personal: The number 10 seeks a partner to become 15. All fives call . . .").

FILLERS

OBJECTIVE TWO:

Students will create slogans, messages, and one-panel cartoons.

PREWRITING:

Students look through newspapers and magazines and write down any "fillers" they see. These include public service announcements, in-house ads, and clip-artwork. Each student will create several original fillers in the boxes on the bottom of a copy of the worksheet on page 56. One example is given.

INTEGRATING THE CURRICULUM

SOCIAL STUDIES:

Fillers can include famous historical quotes, important dates, symbols from the past, or flags of other countries.

SCIENCE:

Fillers can include scientific facts, science formulas, and diagrams of science text chapter concepts.

MATH:

Fillers can include math-oriented facts, math jokes, word problems, and brain teasers.

CLASSIFIED ADS AND FILLERS WORKSHEET

Classified ads, also known as want ads, advertise a variety of things. Listed among these are employment opportunities (help wanted), items for sale, homes for rent, offers to buy, and personal messages. In the boxes below, write several classified ads of your own. Try many different types. Be sure to include a heading, such as WANTED or FOR SALE.

FOR SALE: Two bedroom house with bath. Full kitchen and living room. Fireplace and fenced-in backyard. Dog comes with the yard. Call 555-1369.	

Newspapers and magazines use fillers to fill in extra spaces in their layout when an article is not long enough. Fillers can be public service announcements, interesting quotes, jokes, short poems, small cartoons, or drawings. Fill in the boxes below with a variety of filler material. Try different types of fillers. Be creative, and have fun!

Remember To Recycle! **It's the only way** **for us to** **SURVIVE!**	

Name _____

PUBLISHING
The
NEWSPAPER

★ ★ ★ ★ ★

Students will be writing headlines for their articles throughout this unit. Before beginning their first article, stress to students the importance of writing a good headline. The headline should grab the reader's attention and tell the reader the article's subject, all in a few words. In fact, some of the most effective headlines are the shortest: "War Over!" or "Stock Market Crash!" Headlines also restate names and places, highlight certain words like "new," "fresh," and "hot," and ask a question for emphasis.

Make a transparency of the sample headlines on page 59 or reproduce the page for students. Have students analyze their effectiveness as they guess what might be included in the article that follows. Hint: each headline introduces a famous fairy tale. This is a good time to also note that the fonts used for headlines are different than those used in newspaper articles. Fonts are chosen so that they can be read easily at a distance to grab the reader's attention.

The final headline for an article need not be written until the newspaper is ready to be published. Students should look at all headlines before going "to press" to make sure that they are attention-grabbing and accurate. Stress to students that headlines are never written before the article has been written!

Writing headlines gives students practice in summarizing and locating the main idea of a story or article. A good way to get students to practice this skill is to ask them to exchange articles and write headlines for articles they did not write.

Woodcutter Praised for Daring Rescue

Wolf Fails on Third Demolition Attempt

Beanstalk Crushes Giant

PUMPKIN TO COACH: A FAIRY TALE MAKEOVER

Scientists Question 100-Year Sleep

Tart Thief Captured with Irrefutable Evidence

MASTHEADS

OBJECTIVE:

Students will create different possible titles (mastheads) for the class newspaper.

PREWRITING:

Write newspaper title words on the board (such as Herald, Gazette, Ledger, News, Banner, Constitution, Telegraph, Times, and Press). Each student will use a copy of the worksheet on page 61 on which to design several possible mastheads.

INTEGRATING THE CURRICULUM

SOCIAL STUDIES:

If your newspaper has a social studies emphasis, create a masthead that will reflect it, such as, "The Herald of the Americas."

SCIENCE:

If your newspaper has a science emphasis, create a masthead that will reflect it, such as, "Ecological Times."

MATH:

If your newspaper has a mathematics emphasis, create a masthead that will reflect it, such as, "Mathematics Today."

MASTHEADS

Press   **Times**   **Banner**   **News**

Ledger   **Gazette**   **Herald**   **Telegraph**

These words are often used in the names of newspapers. However, there are many other possible titles. Newspapers also use many different typestyles in their "mastheads" or titles. Some use fancy script, others bold print. Try out several mastheads for your newspaper in the boxes below.

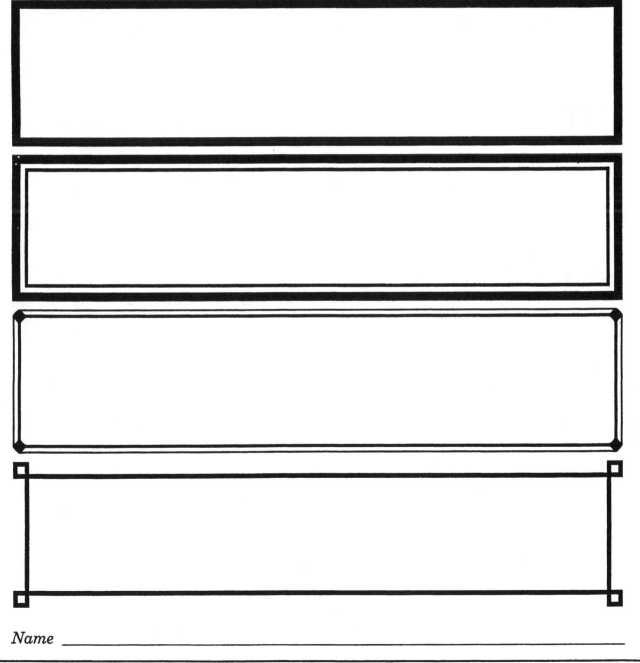

Name _____

PUBLISHING

Once all articles, puzzles, fillers, etc., have been written, publishing decisions must be made. Each group must decide which pieces will be included in the paper. One method for making such decisions is to gather all the pieces of one particular type in a folder. Students read each piece and decide which one(s) to use. Remind the students that each student's work should be represented in the newspaper.

Once all pieces have been selected, students must edit the work carefully for spelling, grammar, and sentence structure. Students can also offer advice to one another for improving their stories. Authors, of course, are free to take this advice or to ignore it. When students are satisfied with their product, the process of typesetting begins.

Using copies of the newspaper layout pattern on page 63, type or print in the text of the stories in columns. Classified ads, fillers, cartoons, ads, survey chart, puzzles, poetry, and mastheads can be used as they are. Other stories must be printed out in column form. If using a computer, set column widths at about $3\frac{1}{4}$". After the material is typed or printed in columns, layout can begin. Use a word-processing program or publication software to create a computer version of your newspaper or follow the instructions below to paste-up your newspaper for printing.

Use standard $8\frac{1}{2}$" x 11" sheets of white paper on which to lay out the paper in columns, including as many pages as necessary. Begin by laying out the pages without affixing the parts first. Although you may be planning to run copies front and back, only use one side during layout. Once you have decided on the information to be placed on specific pages, tape, hot glue, or wax stories, fillers, and headlines to the pages. Include the newspaper's masthead on the top of the first page of the newspaper. Then number the pages. Allow students to complete this entire process by themselves. They will find it quite rewarding.

When all of the pages are ready, use a copy machine to make enough copies for everyone in the class. Display a copy on the bulletin board. Your students' pride will be evident when you see them reading their very own class newspaper!

NEWSPAPER LAYOUT TO REPRODUCE